contents

Real-life case study

This real-life case study highlights some of the issues that surround the debate on same-sex marriage.

case study

Same-sex marriage in California

In June 2008 the state of California in the USA passed a law allowing same-sex marriage for the first time. Same-sex marriage is the marriage between two men or two women. The first couple to be wed after the law was passed were the lead plaintiffs in the case that changed the law, Robin Tyler and Diane Olson. It was a significant moment in America – the ceremony was shown on three local TV networks, and there were more media people than guests at Beverly Hills City Hall, Los Angeles, where the white-tuxedo wearing couple were married.

The two women had been together for 15 years and had known each other for 35 and they had been applying for a marriage licence for 7 years before their wish was finally granted. Supporters of same-sex marriage outside the hall waved rainbow flags and a sign saying simply: "Finally." However, even on Olson and Tyler's happy day there were several angry protesters carrying banners with slogans like "Legalizing gay marriage is legalizing sin" and the fierce debate around same-sex marriage in California continued.

▼ US and world press and protesters crowd around Robin Tyler (left) and Diane Olson at their wedding in June 2008.

Within a year Tyler and Olson were faced with the prospect of their union – and that of thousands of other homosexual couples – being annulled, and their status as a married couple being taken away from them. In May 2009 the Supreme Court of California met to decide to uphold Proposition 8, a ballot in which a small majority of Californians had voted for a measure that stipulated: "only marriage between a man and a woman is valid or recognized in California."

The court's decision did not affect those already married, such as Tyler and Olson.

They, and around 18,000 other homosexual couples who had been married during the six-month period when same-sex marriage was allowed, could stay married. However, the court upheld the ban on any new same-sex weddings. Tyler and Olson and other married homosexual couples in California now lived in a state where same-sex marriage was officially illegal.

In 2010 Californian courts reconsidered the legality of Proposition 8 and many people predict same-sex marriage may once more be legal following 2012 state elections.

▼ In August 2010 supporters of same-sex marriage in California, including Olson and Tyler, celebrated after a federal US judge declared that Proposition 8 was unconstitutional.

viewpoints

"I feel fabulous. I feel in love, I feel giddy, I feel happy. It's like it's not real."
Robin Tyler on her wedding day

"Boys do not marry boys, girls do not marry girls, they never have, whatever they want to do, this is not marriage."
A protester, who gave his name as John, on Tyler and Olson's wedding day

Proposition 8
Born 11/4/08
Dead & Buried 8/4/10

&JUSTICE
ALL

CHAPTER 1

Same-sex relationships

Most people are attracted to members of the opposite sex. Most boys or men are attracted to girls and women, and vice versa. While heterosexual relationships like these are most common, there are also many men and women who are attracted to someone of the same sex as themselves. They are known as homosexual or gay, and homosexual women may refer to themselves as lesbians.

Sexual orientation

Some people say that they knew they were homosexual from a young age; for others it is a realization that comes more gradually. For teenagers the sex hormones that cause puberty and an increase in sexual drive or urges can make it a confusing time. Many people find that they are attracted to members of the same sex for a while and this is perfectly normal. It doesn't mean they are homosexual, though it may. No one knows what makes people heterosexual, homosexual or even bisexual. Whether someone finally realizes they are attracted to the same or to the opposite sex, they are experiencing a normal sexual orientation.

▼ The teenage years are a period of self-discovery about many attitudes and beliefs, and also awareness of sexual orientations.

Coming out

When someone decides to tell other people that they are homosexual it is known as "coming out." Some people find coming out a positive experience, because they can finally express their true feelings. However, it can be a difficult time for many others as a lot of people refuse to accept homosexuality. Prejudice against homosexual people and homosexuality is called homophobia. Like many people who are outside the "norm" at school, college and beyond, some homosexuals face varying degrees of bullying, from name-calling and the frequent use of words like gay being used as insults to more violent forms of physical abuse.

Like other people who are bullied, homosexuals who are bullied are less likely to do well at school, may become depressed or harm themselves. According to Stonewall, a charity that campaigns for a stop to homophobic abuse, almost half of those who have encountered such abuse consider self-harm or even suicide.

▼ "Coming out" is when someone publicly identifies himself as a homosexual.

Attitudes

People's attitudes to homosexuality vary widely. In some countries such as Nigeria and Iran, coming out is incredibly dangerous because homosexual behavior carries the death penalty. In other places, such as Europe and North America, homosexuality is legal and homophobia against the law. However, even in these places, intolerance is still widespread and homosexual people have different legal rights than heterosexual people and issues such as same-sex marriage are still hotly debated.

It's a fact

For anyone who would like support or further information relating to their sexuality, whether they think or know they are heterosexual, homosexual or bisexual, there are many help lines and websites they can visit (see page 47). They should also find out about safer sex messages, such as how to protect against STDs.

In the past

Several ancient cultures accepted and sometimes revered homosexuals. These included Ancient Greeks and Romans, Native American shamans in the Sac and Fox Nations tribes, samurais in Japan, and the Etoro people of Papua New Guinea. However, religions including Christianity and Islam decreed that homosexuality was against God's wishes (see chapter 3). As religion spread its influence globally, so did general acceptance that the Church could punish people, sometimes by death, for being homosexual. Homophobes blamed homosexuals at that time for many

problems, including disease epidemics, for which they were burned at the stake to cleanse them of their so-called polluting influence on the world.

Against the law

In 1533, King Henry VIII of England made the first state law making sex between two men punishable, at that time by hanging. Henry used the law partly to take some power away from the Church. For example, he used spies to find evidence against nuns and monks and once they were found guilty, take monastery lands for the state. This law remained in place until 1861,

▼ Homosexuality was sufficiently acceptable in Ancient Rome for the Emperor Hadrian to have matching marble busts made of himself and his lover Antinous. However, Hadrian lived in a privileged sector of society and for most Romans, especially with the rise in Christianity toward the end of the Empire, homosexuality was not possible.

case study

Oscar Wilde

Oscar Wilde was a famous playwright and poet of the late nineteenth century. He was married to Constance Lloyd but as a homosexual had various affairs with men. After a very public friendship with Lord Alfred Douglas, Lloyd's angry father, the Marquis of Queensberry, accused Wilde of having sex with Douglas. Wilde took Queensberry to court to prove his innocence, but was convicted of earlier acts of indecency with other men. He spent 1895 to 1897 in Reading prison doing hard labor. His health suffered so much that he died just three years after his release.

A statue of Oscar Wilde in his native Dublin. ▶

when punishment was generally imprisonment, although the last execution for the crime in the UK was in 1837. As a result, for hundreds of years homosexual people kept their sexual orientation secret for fear of harassment and arrest by the police, public humiliation at trials or losing their jobs if 'found out'.

Proving homosexuality

In Victorian times, people suspected of being homosexual were often examined by doctors to find proof, and this led the medical profession to search for scientific reasons for homosexuality. Some, for example, claimed that gay men had enlarged areas of their brains normally bigger in women. Finding few physical explanations for homosexuality, Victorian doctors concluded it was a mental illness.

It's a fact

Many homosexuals in the twentieth century were sent to psychiatric hospitals for treatment, such as electric shock therapy and counseling. Homosexuality was classified as a mental illness until 1973 by the US, the World Health Organization until 1990, China until 2001 and India until 2009.

In 1969 the Stonewall Inn and the surrounding area were the site of a series of demonstrations and riots that led to the formation of the modern gay rights movement in the United States.

The struggle for gay rights

An early pioneer for gay rights was German lawyer Magnus Hirschfeld, who founded the Scientific-Humanitarian Committee that campaigned for changes to laws relating to homosexuality in Germany, the Netherlands and Austria in 1897. By the 1920s authorities allowed gay publications and nightclubs in large German cities. The rise of the violently intolerant Nazi regime in the 1930s closed them down and homosexuals were persecuted. For example, homosexuals were imprisoned, forced to wear pink triangles on their clothes and many were beaten to death.

Following the struggle for freedom during World War II, European countries started to give more freedom to homosexual people. For example, in 1967 private meetings between gay men of 21 and over (and not in the military) were deemed no longer illegal.

Stonewall

Many people claim that the gay rights movement truly began in 1969 after the Stonewall Inn, a gay bar in New York, was raided by police, sparking a riot lasting three nights. Hundreds of people fought and protested against being arrested for just having a good time in a club. The publicity triggered the formation of gay and lesbian political groups and encouraged many homosexual people to come out.

The gay rights movement spread and by the mid-1970s the first openly gay politicians were elected in the US, including Nancy Wechsler and Harvey Milk. Gradually gay rights laws started to change. By 1980 it was illegal in the US to discriminate against homosexuals based on their sexual orientation, but laws criminalizing gay sex remained in 12 states including Texas and Georgia up until 2003.

Harvey Milk's nephew, Stuart, accepts a Presidential Medal of Freedom on behalf of Harvey from President Obama. The medal is the highest civilian honor in the United States. President Obama praised Harvey Milk as someone who "saw an imperfect world and set about improving it."

Campaigns for change

The gay rights movement has had different political focuses at different times. For example, in the 1980s a major aim was to increase government funding for research into HIV/AIDS, then especially prevalent amongst the gay community. But one of the most important in the context of equal rights is same-sex marriage. Legal same-sex unions similar to marriage did happen occasionally in the past. For example, in mediaeval France, men could pledge to live together sharing bread, wine and money using "affreremont" or brotherhood contracts. However, more widespread legal acceptance of same-sex unions has only started to happen in some countries at the end of the twentieth century.

viewpoints

"I can only hope that ... gay doctors will come out, the gay lawyers, the gay judges, gay bankers, gay architects ... I hope that every professional gay will say 'enough,' come forward and tell everybody, wear a sign, let the world know. Maybe that will help."
Harvey Milk, 1978

"If homosexuality was the normal way, God would have made Adam and Bruce."
Anita Bryant, gay rights opponent, 1977

summary

▶ Homosexuality is one of a variety of human sexual orientations.

▶ Acceptance of homosexual people depends largely on the religious and cultural views of individuals, groups and governments, and these have varied through time.

▶ Different places have different levels of acceptance and different laws about gay rights.

CHAPTER 2

Why get married?

Almost every culture in history has included some form of marriage and marriage was an essential part of the structure of those societies. It ensured partners in a marriage had rights and that their children would be cared for. It helped societies grow, because men traditionally worked while women cared for the home and children. It also ensured that when someone died their property would be inherited by their children and family. In fact Ancient Hebrew law required a man to marry his deceased brother's widow.

Different forms of marriage

Marriage between a man and a woman used to be more of a contract than a matter of love or choice. In most cultures, families or communities decided who married whom. In the past and still in many cultures today, people may feel under pressure to marry someone from within their own tribe or group. In traditional societies, marriages are arranged by the couple's family. Partners may be chosen to bring social and economic advantages to their two families, although families also try to choose partners who are compatible with each other. In Western societies, young adults usually meet and choose their own partners.

Marriage today

Today some people choose to stay single and many others choose to live together without getting married. They believe that people do not need to get married to have a successful and long-lasting relationship in which they are committed to each other and their families.

A wedding couple ▶ taking their wedding vows in front of friends and family.

Given that some people believe that there is no necessity to get married, why do homosexual couples still want to tie the knot? Some people say they want the security and legal rights that marriage provides for themselves and for their children. Some want to declare their commitment to each other in front of friends, family and the wider community. They want to express their intention to stand together in good times and bad, through all the joys and challenges life brings. Many couples get married simply because they love each other and it feels right.

viewpoints

"Yes I do feel different, more respected by society – because having a ring on my finger shows that I am committed. ... If we are aping heterosexuals, so what? Declaring your love for someone is wonderful, having your loved ones there to witness it is even better."

Shelley Duffy Silas, after marrying her partner, novelist Stella Silas Duffy in 2010

"I'm in a place right now where I don't want to get married. I don't think in this day and age you need to."

Enrique Iglesias, singer (when asked whether he and tennis player Anna Kournikova were married)

▼ Same-sex couples say that getting married gives them a strong sense that they are in a long-term relationship, as it does for heterosexual couples.

13

▲ The rights of children in many cultures depend on whether their parents are married.

Legal aspects of marriage

Heterosexual couples have the advantage of many legal and economic benefits of marriage. However, no matter how long an unmarried couple's relationship has lasted, the law in most places still treats them as separate individuals if that relationship ends. For example, a married person automatically inherits their partner's money and property if that person dies. This is generally not the case for unmarried couples. After an unmarried relationship ends, neither partner has to provide financial support to the other. Unmarried couples may also miss out on tax credits, which are reductions in how much tax they pay the government, financial assistance if their partner is away on military service, medical treatment and other benefits.

Family rights

Unmarried couples are not entitled to other, more personal legal rights either. Legally, children of unmarried parents don't have the same basic rights as children of married couples when it comes to their parents. Neither the parent nor the child has visitation rights if the parents separate and if one parent dies, the second parent has no legal right to care for the child. There are other considerations, too. If a couple is not married they would not automatically get "next-of-kin" status and rights to visit and take important decisions about their partner's medical care in an emergency, even if they had been together for many years and the partner was estranged from the rest of his or her family. They would also be unable to choose how to dispose of their loved one's remains.

DIY documents

Opponents to same-sex marriage argue that same-sex couples, like heterosexual couples who do not marry, can make legal arrangements that give them many of the same rights as married couples. For example, couples can draw up legal documents that grant them child custody or plan how to divide joint property and money in case of a separation. Unmarried couples can also make wills so that if they die, their partner will inherit their home, money and pensions. However, these arrangements would not cover all the benefits afforded to other couples by their married status, such as next-of-kin status in times of emergency.

▼ In an emergency, only people who have next-of-kin status may be allowed at a patient's bedside.

case study

Banned from her partner's bedside

In February 2007, Janice Langbehn, her partner of 18 years Lisa Pond and their three adopted children, aged 9, 11 and 13 were about to set off on a cruise from Florida when Pond collapsed. Florida did not recognize same-sex partnerships so as Pond lay dying of a brain hemorrhage in the hospital, Langbehn was fighting to see her. She said afterwards that she and their children were only allowed to see Pond briefly before she died 24 hours later. "I have this deep sense of failure for not being at Lisa's bedside when she died," Langbehn said. "How I get over that I don't know, or if I ever do."

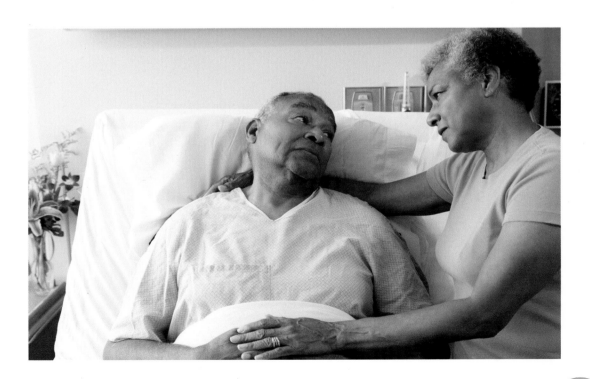

Civil unions and partnerships

In many countries same-sex unions are not allowed at all, but in some places, such as the UK, same-sex couples are now able to register a formal commitment to one another in a domestic or civil partnership, also known as a civil union. This gives them legal recognition for their relationship and many of the same rights and responsibilities as married couples.

There are some differences. For example marriage ceremonies for opposite-sex couples can be either religious or civil, whereas a civil partnership can only be created by a civil ceremony. A partnership is formed when the couple signs papers and it doesn't have to be a public ceremony, whereas a marriage happens when the couple exchanges spoken words and signs the register. Denmark established legal same-sex civil partnerships in 1989 and was soon followed by several other mostly Northern European countries during the 1990s.

viewpoints

"I don't want to be married. David and I are not married. Let's get that right. We have a civil partnership. What is wrong with Proposition 8 is that they went for marriage. Marriage is going to put a lot of people off. It's the word marriage."
Singer Sir Elton John speaking about his civil partnership, 2008

"I believe that adopting same-sex marriage would be likely to improve the well-being of gay and lesbian households and their children."
David Blankenhorn, founder of the Institute for American Values

▼ Two men signing the register at their Civil Partnership Ceremony, watched by the Registrar.

case study

Choosing marriage in Iceland

Iceland's Prime Minister, Johanna Sigurdardottir, and her long-term partner, Jonina Leosdottir, took part in a civil union ceremony in 2002. It gave them the same rights and benefits as married heterosexual couples, but they still wanted to have a full "marriage." In June 2010 Iceland's parliament voted to make marriage a gender-neutral institution that includes "man and man" and "woman and woman" in its definitions of marriage. This replaced the former system of registered partnerships and granted homosexual couples all the benefits and obligations of marriage, including adoption. Sigurdardottir and Leosdottir changed their civil union into a marriage on the very first day that the new law came into force.

Johanna Sigurdardottir is Iceland's first openly homosexual Prime Minister.

Civil unions vs. marriage

While many homosexual couples are satisfied with the option of a civil union or partnership, others feel aggrieved that they cannot have a marriage. One reason for this is that although a civil partnership gives homosexual couples most of the same legal rights, it does not give all of them. There are often differences to do with the right to adopt children. For example, in Latin America same-sex civil unions are legal in Uruguay and some states in Brazil but these contracts do not give homosexual couples the right to adopt.

Some supporters of same-sex marriage also say that civil partnerships and unions do not have the same symbolic status as a marriage. They say that it is a second-class status and that civil unions should be replaced by gender-neutral marriage.

Same-sex unions in the US

In America different states have different policies. In 1996 Congress brought in the Defense of Marriage Act, which prompted most states to define marriage as purely heterosexual and to not recognise same-sex marriages from other states.

However, several states had different ideas. For example, California started to give licences for same-sex domestic partnerships, with equivalent legal rights as married heterosexual couples in 2003. In 2004 officials in San Francisco, a city in California with a high proportion of homosexual people in its population, started to issue same-sex marriage licences, but these were not recognized by other places in the same state! In early 2008 state judges ruled that it was illegal to limit marriage to a man and a woman, by late 2008 reversed its decision (see pages 4-5) and in 2010 reversed it again, each time because of public pressure. In 2011, New York became the largest state to legalize gay marriage.

Around the world

More countries are gradually finding that there is no reason not to give homosexual people equal marriage rights. The first official same-sex marriage happened in 2001 in the Netherlands, and countries including Canada, Spain, South Africa and Argentina had changed their marriage laws by the end of 2010 (see box on page 19). In some places there are still different laws about marriage within a country. For example, civil unions are allowed in Mexico, but gay marriage, which gives homosexual couples extra rights such as adoption, is only legal in Mexico City. In spite of these major developments, in some places around the world same-sex marriage and homosexuality are still subjects of fierce debate and are issues that raise strong feelings on both sides.

▼ Children joining in a protest against a ruling by the Spanish parliament in 2005 to allow same-sex couples to marry and adopt children in Madrid. The banner reads "Marriage = A man and a woman."

▲ In Mexico City in 2009 marriage was defined for the first time as a free union between two people, not just a man and a woman. In the rest of the country, same-sex marriage is recognized but not performed.

It's a fact

Same-sex marriage around the world

Place	Year legalized
Netherlands	2001
Belgium	2003
Massachusetts	2004
Canada	2005
Spain	2005
South Africa	2006
Connecticut	2008
Mexico City, Mexico	2009
Norway	2009
Sweden	2009
Iowa, Vermont, Maine and District of Columbia	2009
Portugal	2010
Iceland	2010
Argentina	2010
New Hampshire	2010
New York	2011

summary

▶ Marriage gives both partners in a couple legal rights and responsibilities to each other and their children.

▶ Most countries in the world do not offer marriage to homosexual couples.

▶ In some countries, homosexual couples can enter into a civil union or partnership which gives them most of the same rights and responsibilities as marriage.

CHAPTER 3

Religious rite or civil right?

In many countries the main obstacle to same-sex marriage is religious objection. Many religious leaders and followers object to homosexual marriage because they believe that their religion tells them homosexuality is sinful. They say that homosexuality is against the Christian Bible, the Muslim Qur'an and other holy books.

There are passages in sacred texts that condemn homosexual acts and negative passages about homosexuality in the scriptures and other holy books. For example, sentences like "If a man lies with a man as one lies with a woman, both of them have done what is detestable. They must be put to death; their blood will be on their own heads," from the Bible (Leviticus 20:13) lead to the Catholic Church's tough stance on homosexuality and its call for homosexual Catholics to live chaste lives.

Religious interpretations

As with most debates on ethical issues, one of the main problems for religious leaders is how religious books should be interpreted. In modern society religious people do many things that are supposedly forbidden by their holy texts. For example, the Bible tells Christians they should not wear mixed fibers, eat shellfish or let disabled people into temples, but none of these edicts is followed to the letter. And there are passages in the Bible that some

▼ The Pope is the leader of the Catholic Church, which teaches that while homosexuality is not sinful, homosexual acts are. However, there are ordinary Catholics who do not agree with this edict.

Archbishop Desmond Tutu, who retired from public service in 2010, tirelessly campaigned for equal rights not only for black people, but also for homosexual people in South Africa and worldwide.

interpret as showing same-sex unions as normal, "... Jonathan became one in spirit with David and he loved him as himself." In fact, many people do not believe they have to take every word of their holy text literally in order to be a follower of their particular faith. They say that texts written long ago were written for that particular time and were never intended to be taken literally and believe that such texts are open to interpretation because they were meant to offer guidance only.

Range of opinions

Within every religious movement there is a great range of opinion. Some Christians condemn homosexuality but many others accept it, regarding homosexuality as a sexual orientation which is normal and natural for some adults. Many religious leaders welcome homosexuals to their religious communities. For example, the Anglican communities in North America,

Europe, Australia, New Zealand and southern Africa generally do not regard homosexuality as sinful. However, in the majority of Africa and the West Indies, and in other places where there are evangelical Anglican groups, Anglicans believe that homosexuality should be condemned.

viewpoints

"Everyone is an insider, there are no outsiders – whatever their beliefs, whatever their color, gender or sexuality."
Archbishop Desmond Tutu, 2004

"Transsexuals and homosexuals will never enter the kingdom of heaven and it is not me who says this, but Saint Paul. ... It may not be their fault, but acting against nature and the dignity of the human body is an insult to God."
Leading Roman Catholic Cardinal Javier Lozano Barragán, 2009

▲ A traditional religious view of marriage is one that promotes the idea of the nuclear family – a family with two parents, one male and one female, and their children. Today many families do not fit this model.

The meaning of marriage

While many religious people accept homosexuals into their communities, they draw the line at allowing same-sex marriages or unions. The reason traditionally given for this, for example by the Catholic Church, is that marriage is for procreation, to create and care for children. Unlike the offspring of most other species of animals in the world, children need to be looked after for a long time before they are ready to look after themselves. Traditionally marriage provided a way of helping parents fulfill their duties and responsibilities to their children. The argument of many religions is that since same-sex couples cannot produce children, same-sex marriage should not be permitted.

Modern marriage

Supporters of same-sex marriage say that marriage today is not simply about having children. Since the 1960s and the advent of new forms of contraception such as the Pill, couples have been able to choose not to have children, although some Catholic couples follow decrees from Catholic leaders in Rome saying that artificial contraception should not be used. The marriages of heterosexual couples who choose not to or are unable to have children are still considered valid. The idea of natural law, where only a man and a woman can have a child, has also been challenged by medical developments to help childless couples have children, such as donor insemination and surrogacy.

A religious rite

Another argument that some religious opponents to same-sex unions give is that marriage is a religious rite and that the word "marriage" should only be used in the context of religion. In Islam, for example, marriage is considered to be a gift from God or a kind of service to God, and in Judaism marriage is believed to have been introduced by God. Even in countries where civil partnerships are offered, most ceremonies have had to be secular, or non-religious. Religious aspects of heterosexual weddings, such as hymns or Bible readings, are not allowed in most civil partnerships in order to preserve the definition of religious marriage as the union of a man and a woman.

viewpoints

"Marriage is holy, while homosexual acts go against the natural moral law. Homosexual acts close the sexual act to the gift of life. ... Under no circumstances can they be approved."
Statement from the Vatican, the center of the Catholic faith

"Religions are not immune to a basic law of history: Everything changes. Over time, some faiths become more conservative, others more liberal."
Ron Grossman, journalist

For most Catholics, marriage is a religious rite reserved for a man and a woman only and intended for procreation, or the production of children.

▲ Richard and Mildred Loving's wedding in 1958 led to their arrest and eventually to a change in law in 1967 to allow interracial marriage in America.

Is marriage a civil right?

Many supporters of same-sex marriage say that marriage is not so much a religious as a civil rights issue. Civil rights are the rights of individuals not to be discriminated against in areas of their life, such as employment, voting in elections etc. In ethical debates about same-sex marriage supporters say that laws prohibiting any type of same-sex marriage are discriminatory. They are against an individual's civil rights and no different than laws in the past that prevented inter-racial couples from marrying. These laws have been overturned, for example in the US

viewpoints

"I have fought too hard and too long against discrimination based on race and colour not to stand up against discrimination based on sexual orientation. I've heard the reasons for opposing civil marriage for same-sex couples. Cut through the distractions, and they stink of the same fear, hatred and intolerance I have known in racism and in bigotry."
US Rep. John Lewis, a leader of the black civil rights movement, in the *Boston Globe*, 2003

"The comparison with slavery is a stretch, in that some slave masters were gay, in that gays were never called three-fifths human in the Constitution and in that they did not require the Voting Rights Act to have the right to vote."
Jesse Jackson, American civil rights activist and Baptist minister, Harvard, 2004

in 1967, and today many people believe that it is just a matter of time before laws preventing same-sex couples from marrying are overturned, too.

In South Africa for example, people fought long and hard to end apartheid, the system of discrimination whereby white people had many more rights than other people, especially black people. After the apartheid regime was toppled in 1990 the new constitution in South Africa made discrimination illegal and there was a clause in the constitution that also made discrimination based on sexual identity illegal. In 2005 South Africa amended its marriage laws to include same-sex unions.

Same-sex marriage and discrimination

Some opponents of same-sex marriage claim that gay rights cannot be equated with racial equality because while people do not choose their ethnicity, they say that people choose to be homosexual and that a chosen behavior does not deserve special legal protection. Supporters of same-sex marriage say that homosexuals no more choose their sexual orientation than they choose their gender or their ethnicity; it is simply who they are. And if this is the case, to discriminate against someone because of their homosexuality is the same as any other form of discrimination, including sexism and racism. They believe that just as inter-racial marriage is no longer regarded as a subject for ethical debate for most people, the same will be true of same-sex marriage in the future.

▼ A same-sex couple is married in the chapel of Robben Island Museum, which was once the prison where Nelson Mandela and other black civil rights protesters were held by the South African government during the second half of the twentieth century.

Legal systems have religious roots

Legal systems in many countries have religious roots and religion has had a strong influence on marriage laws in particular. For example the legal system in the US evolved out of the laws contained in the Bible and religious texts are the basis for Islamic and Jewish family law. Some people believe that this gives religious authorities the right to influence law-makers in order to prevent same-sex marriage today. They say that if religious freedom is a legal right, then it is their belief that it goes against the religious freedom of the majority to have to recognize a relationship that those people consider sinful.

case study

Testing Europe on gay marriage

In June 2010 Horst Michael Schalk and Johann Franz Kopf took their case to the European Court of Human Rights. They argued by not allowing them the right to marry, their home country of Austria was violating their right to be free from discrimination and to privacy and family life, as guaranteed by the European Convention on Human Rights.

In 2010 Austria was one of the 40 member nations of the Council of Europe that did not allow same-sex marriage; the other seven member nations already allowed it. If the Court had agreed that Austria was violating Schalk and Kopf's rights, the people of other member states such as Russia, Italy or Poland would also have been able to successfully challenge the ban on same-sex marriage in their countries. The Court felt this meant they were voting to effectively force member states to legalize same-sex marriage and Schalk and Kopf lost their case. However, the vote was close and supporters believe it was a test case that will lead to full equality for same-sex families in the future.

▼ Horst Michael Schalk on the right discusses his complaint against Austria with his legal counsellor at the European Court of Human Rights in Strasbourg, France.

▲ Opponents of same-sex marriage outside the State House in Boston, Massachusetts, in January 2007 where judges were voting to decide whether the issue of laws banning gay marriage should be put to a people's vote, or referendum. The eventual vote was 151 votes opposed to the proposed referendum against 45 in favor.

Marriage as a legal contract

Supporters of same-sex marriage counter such arguments by saying that laws preventing homosexual marriage derive from religious texts and have no place in a country where the laws are secular (non-religious). In the US, for example, the constitution is based on the principle of separation of church and state and this is an integral part of American government. If marriage by the state is a secular activity and a legal contract, the government cannot keep or make laws just because a religion says it should.

They say that allowing marriage rights to same-sex couples would not force religious leaders to perform these ceremonies or hold them in their places of worship. People of faith would be free to have different views on those marriages to the government, as they do already. For example, the US government recognizes the second marriages of all previously divorced couples and gives them the same rights as every other married couple. On the other hand, the Catholic Church is free to rule that it considers second marriages invalid because it does not sanction divorce.

People of faith

The idea of same-sex marriages and civil unions falling under the category of state-sanctioned partnerships has implications for homosexual couples of faith. What do same-sex Hindu, Sikh, Jewish, Muslim or Christian couples do if they want to marry in their place of worship and according to the principles of their faith?

Some religious communities that do not wish to offer same-sex marriages to their congregations fear that changes in laws offering civil unions or partnerships will one day force them to do so. In 2010 in the UK, an amendment was added to the law on civil partnership that allowed same-sex wedding ceremonies to take place in places of worship if a religious group

◀ Rev. Alicia Heath-Toby stands next to her partner Saundra Toby-Heath (right) at the Liberation in Truth Unity Fellowship Church, where she is pastor in New Jersey. In New Jersey homosexual couples cannot marry in their places of worship.

permitted it. Some Jewish Rabbis immediately said they would conduct such services and many senior church officials supported the move. Many traditionalists in the UK and elsewhere fear that changes in laws like this will not only mean that the differences between civil unions and marriages will become blurred, but might also lead to churches closing one day. Their argument is that since same-sex marriages are allowed in places of worship by law, they might face legal challenges by couples who take them to court under anti-discrimination laws.

Religious support for same-sex marriage

In some countries, there are religious leaders who have conducted their own wedding ceremonies for homosexual couples, or offer blessings after a civil union. British Quakers have been celebrating same-sex unions through special acts of worship since 1987 and a Quaker same-sex commitment follows a similar format to a Quaker wedding with the couple exchanging vows within their worshipping community. In 2005 in the US the Episcopal Church and the Evangelical Lutheran Church started to celebrate same-sex marriages in church. In the same year the United Church of Christ, which has 1.3 million followers, became the largest Christian Church in the United States to support and offer same-sex marriage.

v i e w p o i n t s

"I really wasn't comfortable with the idea of going to a civil registrar: it's not what marriage is about for us. It's a solemn and binding commitment in the presence of God. Without some recognition of that religious element, it certainly put me off the idea of getting married."
Chris Campbell, a UK Quaker in a long-term homosexual relationship with a Roman Catholic

"It is a step towards forcing churches to conduct same-sex unions that would go against their beliefs. Changing the law will further blur the distinction between marriage and what the Government put forward as a purely secular ceremony."
Andrea Williams of the Christian Legal Centre speaking of the UK government lifting the ban on religious premises holding same-sex partnerships

It's a fact

The Quakers – or Religious Society of Friends – view marriage as the Lord's work and not that of priests or magistrates. They believe that religious ceremonies should recognize committed relationships regardless of the genders involved. In their book on Quaker faith "same-sex marriages can be prepared, celebrated, witnessed, recorded and reported to the State, as opposite-sex marriages are." The Quakers have formally acknowledged same-sex relationships since the 1960s and are the first religious group in the UK to approve marriages for homosexuals.

s u m m a r y

▶ Some religions teach that marriage should only happen between a man and a woman.

▶ Some people believe that same-sex marriage is a civil right.

▶ Some religions carry out same-sex marriages or blessings after a civil union for followers in their places of worship.

CHAPTER 4

Families and children

It is possible for same-sex couples to have children in several different ways. Some couples have children from a previous heterosexual relationship and some adopt children whose parents cannot bring them up. Lesbian couples can have children through donor insemination, which uses sperm from a donor to help one of the women in the couple to become pregnant. Surrogacy is when another woman carries and gives birth to a baby for a couple who want to have a child, using donated eggs and sperm. Co-parenting is when, for example, a lesbian woman and a homosexual man combine their eggs and sperm (usually using an insemination kit) to parent a child.

It's a fact

Barrie and Tony Drewitt-Barlow, of Danbury, Essex, hit the headlines in 1999 when their twin daughters Aspen and Saffron were born to a surrogate mother in California and became the first British children to be registered as having two fathers and no mother.

Legal issues

The laws about same-sex couples having children vary around the world. For example, Portugal passed a law to legalize same-sex marriage in 2010, but rejected

▼ Noah, 22 months, and Mackenlie, 9 years, pose with their parents, Hazel (left) and Donna Jensen-Wysinger in Salt Lake City. Hazel is the biological parent of Noah, and Donna is the biological parent of Mackenlie, and the two lesbians cross-adopted each other's child to legally form their family.

proposals to allow homosexual couples to adopt. In the USA, surrogacy for same-sex couples is legal in some states, while in others it is considered a criminal act. Some same-sex couples who are banned from adopting or using surrogates in their own country go elsewhere to become parents.

In the case of co-parenting the couple may choose to legally agree to some issues before the baby is born, such as how much time the child will spend with each parent and how much each partner will pay for the child's upbringing, in case of disagreements later.

case study

Israeli parents bring baby home from India

Israel doesn't allow same-sex parents to legally adopt a baby or use the services of a surrogate mother so Yonatan and Omer Gher started their family in India. Although India criminalizes homosexuality, it does allow same-sex couples to hire a surrogate mother to deliver their child there. So, after a long search, Yonatan and Omer found a suitable surrogate in Mumbai and their son Evyatar was conceived using sperm from Yonatan and eggs from an anonymous donor in a fertility clinic.

They returned to Israel during the pregnancy but kept in touch with the mother by e-mail and returned to India in time for their son's birth. Before they could take him home, the Israeli government required the new parents to do a DNA test to prove their paternity. Back in Israel, the walls of the couple's home are covered in pictures of their baby boy and they do shifts to take care of him round the clock. They hope to return to Mumbai and use the same donor to have a brother or sister for Evyatar.

Omer and Yonatan Gher chose their son's name – Evyatar – from the Bible. It means "more fathers" in Hebrew.

The ethical debates around same-sex parenting get to the heart of what being a family really means and what it is that children most need from any parents or carers.

v i e w p o i n t s

"It was normal to me, it was all I knew. I remember one day in school a guy came in and said 'your parents are lesbians.' But before that I'd never put a word to it. I went home and said to my mothers 'are you lesbians?' I think I was eight or nine."
Evan Barry, a 23-year-old from Dublin who has two mothers

"A baby is not a trophy – the child's welfare has to be considered. These children are more likely to experiment with same-sex relationships. They're more likely to be confused and hurt."
Dale O'Leary, author of One Man, One Woman: A Catholic's Guide to Defending Marriage

Moms or dads?

Opponents of same-sex families think that children need one parent of each sex to develop properly and that the traditional ideal of a nuclear family should be followed as closely as possible. They believe that children need both male and female influences and if a child's natural parents are unable to look after them, the child should only be adopted into a family where there are both mother and father figures. Some think that while homosexual relationships should be accepted, the law should encourage the ideal of the nuclear family by making it illegal for same-sex couples to have families by adoption or other means.

For many other people, the sex of a child's parents is not the issue. The real issue for them is whether those parents will nurture and love the child and give it the stability it needs, and both men and women are

It's a fact

There are about 600,000 same-sex couples living in America. Two-fifths of same-sex couples in the US aged 22 to 55 are raising children. In total they are raising more than 250,000 children under the age of 18.

equally capable of this. They say that society is changing and the traditional model of the nuclear family with a married mother and father is no longer the only acceptable alternative. There are many different kinds of families around us, including single-parent families, step-families and those in which children are brought up by their grandparents. In a world where there is a shortage of foster parents and there are many children waiting for adoption, many people ask why shouldn't homosexual couples be able to offer these children the stable and loving home they need?

Gay parents, gay kids?

Another issue in this debate has to do with sexuality. Some people think that children of same-sex couples are significantly more likely to be homosexual themselves. They argue that, if a child's main role models are his or her parents, growing up in a same-sex family will give the child a one-sided view of sexual orientation. However, most of the world's homosexual men and women have heterosexual parents, and according to the American Psychological Association, numerous research studies have shown that children from same-sex households describe themselves as heterosexual in roughly the same proportion as from more conventional families. Most scientists agree that some babies seem to be simply born with a predisposition to homosexuality.

▼ Whether a family interacts successfully and is happy and fulfilled depends on the mutual understanding and respect of individuals within it, regardless of their gender or sexual orientation.

Stress and stigma?

Some people say that same-sex couples should not become parents because of the bullying and problems that their children can face. Homophobic language and behaviour are still common in many places and when a gay couple has a child, that child can become a victim of this prejudice, too. As much as they love their families, some young people may keep quiet about their same-sex parents to avoid bullying or they might find it difficult having them come to school for parent-teacher meetings or sports days. Some young people could feel isolated and threatened by other people's abusive attitudes and behavior towards their parents' homosexuality.

Attitudes and acceptance

There are people who do not accept that same-sex parents can offer children a happy, stable home. Some same-sex couples believe that by living in a place as a successful same-sex family, they can help to overcome such prejudice. Others choose to live in places that are more accepting. For example, cities tend to be more diverse than rural areas and more respectful of non-traditional families.

Some children who have been teased or bullied about having same-sex parents say that they have learned to be more empathetic and accepting of people who are different because they know how it feels to be unfairly judged. For some, it increases their respect for their parents who have been brave enough to be true to their sexuality in the face of criticism. What matters is whether or not their parents have always been there for them, not their parents' sexual orientation.

▼ Bullies often attack things they don't understand or that they perceive as "different," and as having same-sex parents is something many people are unfamiliar with, some children of same-sex families face bullying at school.

<h1 style="text-align:center">case study</h1>

Growing up with two moms

Jeff DeGroot is a young adult who was raised by two lesbian mothers in Oregon. He never felt he missed out on having a father and his parents did all the things people might expect a father to do, like playing baseball with him and taking him hiking. His mothers, Elisabeth and Meg, always made sure that he had several male role models in his life so that no one could suggest he was missing out on anything by not having a dad.

He had fun deciding what to call his parents: "If I'm on one side of the house and I want to talk to my biological mom, I'll yell, 'Mother.' If Meg says, 'Yes?' I'll say, 'No, other mother!'"

Jeff grew up in Corvallis, Oregon, a college town in a state where same-sex couples were generally more accepted and he did not have a problem with teasing or bullying from his classmates or community. In fact some of Jeff's friends thought he was cool for having two lesbian moms and would say, "Oh, you got two moms? I gotta meet them!"

What upsets one of his mothers, Elisabeth, most, is critics who say that children of same-sex couples will grow up physiologically damaged. "'That makes me mad. I know better. There's Jeff," she says.

▲ Maureen Kilian smiles as Cindy Meneghin asks her to marry her as their son Josh looks on. The New Jersey couple were celebrating a Supreme Court ruling that homosexuals are entitled to the same rights as heterosexuals.

summary

► Same-sex couples can have children in several different ways, for example by adoption, artificial insemination, surrogacy and co-parenting.

► Different countries around the world have different laws regarding adoption, surrogacy and other methods of same-sex parenting.

► Many studies show that there is no real difference between children of same-sex couples and heterosexual couples.

CHAPTER 5

Effects on society

Another debate that centers on homosexual marriage is how it will affect the structures of society and everyday life. Will same-sex marriage, as some fear, change the status and expectations of marriage and bring an increase in divorce rates and fractured families? Or will it, as others believe, serve to strengthen the institution of marriage and bring a range of benefits to individuals and communities?

A slippery slope...

Some opponents of same-sex marriage fear that if countries allow it, marriage could be transformed into a variety of relationship contracts between two, three

◄ Barrie and Tony Drewitt-Barlow (front and back left) at the church baptism of their son Orlando and twins Jasper and Dallas in 2010, attended also by the children's surrogate mothers. Many people believe that public acceptance of same-sex couples' commitment to union and to their unusual family set-ups might be improved by allowing more same-sex marriages.

or more people of the same or different sexes. They say that without a firm definition of marriage, options might become endless and that these non-traditional families could break down the family values upon which society is built. Many people question this logic. They point to the fact that, in some cultures, including the Mormons, polygamous marriages have been around for centuries, well before any same-sex marriages, but remain a minority choice.

Divorce

Another criticism of same-sex marriage is that it could increase the rates of divorce. Organizations such as the Family Research Council (FRC), which opposes same-sex marriage, claim that same-sex couples divorce sooner than heterosexual couples. To support this, they present official data on marriage from across the USA, involving tens of thousands of heterosexual people, showing that around 70 per cent stay married for 10 or more years. They contrast this with a Gay/Lesbian Consumer Online Census of under 8,000 people from 2003/2004 showing that most homosexual relationships last less than three years.

The conclusion they draw from this is that homosexual partners in a same-sex marriage would not insist on sexual fidelity and that by having affairs outside marriage, this would lessen the idea of marriage as a long-term commitment and make it more likely that heterosexual couples would be unfaithful too, leading to more divorces.

People supporting same-sex marriage say this evidence does not prove same-sex marriage leads to more divorce. They argue that data used by the FRC are not comparable as they contrast government statistics with online answers from a small questionnaire, and say that they also prove nothing. For example, they cite the fact that, since same-sex marriage became legal in 2004, divorce rates in Massachusetts have remained some of the lowest in the US. They point out that overall divorce rates are increasing in many countries that do not allow same-sex marriage, because this reflects other changes in society.

It's a fact

Divorce rate statistics should be read with caution. In the US around 50 per cent of all marriages end in divorce, but in India the figure is around 1 per cent. This does not mean that Indians are more likely to be happily married, but that divorce is less acceptable culturally than in the USA. The divorce rate is falling in countries such as the UK. This is partly a consequence of people getting married when they are older and more committed to each other, but partly because fewer people overall are getting married.

viewpoints

"Americans will see that when lesbians and gay men are given access to most of the rights and obligations of civil marriage, the sky will not fall and the institution of marriage will be even stronger."
Evan Wolfson, American gay rights lawyer

"Homosexuals are not monogamous. They want to destroy the institution of marriage. It [same-sex marriage] will destroy marriage. It will destroy the Earth."
Dr. James Dobson, from Focus on the Family

Society stability

Some people believe that more widespread same-sex marriage could enhance the stability of society that others feel is at risk. If more homosexual people were allowed to marry, this could discourage promiscuity, and encourage stable relationships and the strong family values that conservatives want. Allowing married same-sex couples to adopt could help society by taking more children from foster care into stable family settings. UK statistics from 2010 suggest that three-quarters of children who are still in foster care by their sixteenth birthday will have a criminal conviction in the future.

A dangerous lifestyle?

There are concerns amongst some that same-sex marriage could expose more people to a homosexual lifestyle that they consider to be dangerous. Their reasoning is that by making same-sex marriage as acceptable as heterosexual marriage, homosexuality will become more widespread. Their argument rests on the notion that some homosexual people behave in ways that can endanger their own health and the health of others, such as having unprotected sex with several partners and thus risking the spread of diseases such as hepatitis and HIV/AIDS. HIV/AIDS is the world's most deadly infectious disease and the fourth biggest killer worldwide.

It is widely accepted that some homosexual people have higher rates of depression, suicide risk and lower life expectancy than most heterosexual people. Research has shown that the trauma of experiencing homophobic bullying is a significant cause of these statistics (see page 7).

A poster in Niger warns of the dangers of AIDS (SIDA). It stresses that the disease can be spread by heterosexuals and that condoms, abstinence from sex and fidelity (having fewer partners) can help protect against AIDS.

Other people disagree with the idea that same-sex marriage will increase risky homosexual behavior. They argue that potentially health-damaging promiscuous behavior exists in heterosexuals, too, and that heterosexual AIDS/HIV affects millions of heterosexuals in addition to homosexuals. They suggest that, if people think homosexuals are more likely to be promiscuous, this could be an argument in favor of gay marriage, to encourage stability in relationships. Psychological problems such as depression are always more likely in people who feel outside of the mainstream society and face prejudice and homophobia, something that might be improved if same-sex marriage became more mainstream.

case study

Changing sex for society's sake in Iran

Iran's society is based in Islam and in general the country is very traditional in its view of gender – people should be either male or female heterosexuals. Homophobia is common. For example, in 2008 Iranian religious cleric Hojatol Kariminia said: "Homosexuals are doing something unnatural and against religion. It is clearly stated in our Islamic law that such behavior is not allowed because it disrupts the social order."

People found guilty of having sex with someone of their own gender face public beating and sometimes execution. Perhaps surprisingly, transgender people – those who believe their true sexuality is opposite to the gender they were born with – are tolerated by the Iranian state. If officially diagnosed as transgender, people receive government support to have sex-changing surgery that transforms them physically into the opposite gender. Then their gender is changed on their birth certificate and they can even get married legally. The state considers this type of gender change much more acceptable and better for society than homosexuality.

Maryam Khatoon Molkara (left, with her husband Mohammed) is a transgender woman who, in the 1980s, was the first Iranian man to have an officially approved sex-change operation. Now she runs a center in Tehran that aims to help transsexuals in Iran and the region.

▲ Wedding receptions can be phenomenally expensive, lavish occasions that provide work for many people. Same-sex marriages and civil unions are a relatively new and affluent market targeted by the wedding industry worldwide.

Making money from same-sex marriage

Same-sex marriages generate money in different ways for any society. In places such as the UK or US, the shared household income of married people is used to find out how much state help the government should give them. For example, the government might provide healthcare benefits to individuals but not to married couples because they can partly support each other financially. By allowing same-sex marriages, governments can save money on benefits. In 2003, a study estimated that New Jersey could save $61 million each year by upgrading same-sex unions from domestic partnerships to marriages.

Same-sex marriage also brings money to places through the wedding industry. This includes the businesses that make a wedding happen, from jewelery and dress shops, to caterers, hotels and photographers. The average cost of a wedding is around $21,000, not including a honeymoon and the income from a same-sex marriage is often greater than its heterosexual equivalent. The average

disposable income of homosexual people is higher than that of heterosexual people because typically they do not have families to spend money on. Many people refer to this money as the pink pound or dollar.

Chasing the pink pound

Researchers in 2008 estimated that, for California, legalizing same-sex marriages could bring an extra $700 million to the wedding industry and also $65 million in marriage fees to the state government within three years. This was never tested as the state changed its mind over legalization (see page 5). However, in the District of

It's a fact

Individuals in same-sex couples contribute to the United States economy: 71 percent of them are employed compared with 65 per cent of individuals in married couples.

Pink Mountain tour company in Nepal offers same-sex weddings at the base of Mount Everest as part of Nepal's drive to welcome and make money from homosexual tourists.

case study

Gay tourism in Nepal

Homosexuality is not well tolerated in Asia in general, but Nepal plans to become a regional leader in tourism specifically aimed at homosexual people. Tourism is the biggest industry in Nepal yet has been severely affected both by the global economic crisis and also by civil war.

Although Nepal only made homosexuality legal in 2007, its government plans to legalize same-sex weddings in 2011. Sunil Pant is a homosexual member of Nepal's parliament who has fought for gay rights in Nepal. He has also set up a specialist travel agency especially for homosexual tourists called Pink Mountain. The first unofficial same-sex wedding took place in August 2010, and a high-profile wedding of an Indian prince and his partner is planned.

Columbia, revenue from same-sex marriages following legalization there turned out to be much lower than expected. There are several reasons for this, such as the global economic crisis and the fact that for some same-sex couples, marriage is merely a legal formality of a union that has already been celebrated. Nevertheless, in some places worldwide wedding planners and tourism authorities are trying to encourage same-sex weddings in the hope of a bigger share of the pink pound or dollar.

summary

▶ There is a debate over the impact of same-sex marriage on divorce rates, the stability of society and the incidence of dangerous homosexual behavior.

▶ Same-sex marriage can bring social benefits such as legally adopting children in care and economic benefits for the wedding industry.

CHAPTER 6

Into the future

Are there too many cultural and religious obstacles to same-sex marriage in some places for it to ever become legal? Is the idea of equal rights for same-sex couples now sufficiently established that same-sex marriage will become the norm worldwide? Predicting the future of this debate is very tricky given the wide acceptance gap between different people and countries.

Almost there?

The histories of controversial topics, such as the abolition of slavery and winning equal rights for women, show that some laws and institutions take a long time to change. They often change in one place following key events in another. For example, Stonewall (see page 10) triggered a change in gay rights in the US and worldwide.

Many people feel that same-sex marriage could soon be legalized across European countries, especially since the 2010 case at the European Court of Human Rights (see page 26) dismissed only narrowly a gay couple's claim that Austria took away their human rights by not letting them marry.

The desire for a change in homosexual equality was already there before the Stonewall riot, but it is commemorated today because it was the start of public awareness of this issue. ▶

CHARLES SCRIBNER'S SONS · PUBLISHERS

S THE STONEWALL INN
where pride began
53 christopher st. @ 7th ave.
www.thestonewallinn.net

Other people question whether attitudes have really changed. Across the states the public consistently votes against same-sex marriage even in places where courts have made it legal, based on interpretations of the American constitution. In Texas the Board of Education plans to revise school textbooks based on the political views of the state's ruling Republican Party. In their 2010 Platform document, the party said that "Homosexuality must not be presented as an acceptable 'alternative' lifestyle in our public education and policy, nor should 'family' be redefined to include homosexual 'couples.'"

At least there is debate about same-sex marriage in the USA, which is not the case in other parts of the world. For example, in Kenya in 2010 rumors of a possible gay wedding in the town of Mtwapa began a wave of homophobic violence which was condoned by the government.

▼ In 2010 human rights protesters worldwide, including here in South Africa, criticized Malawi's decision to sentence a same-sex couple to 14 years hard labor.

case study

Predicting the US future

In 2009, Nate Silver, a data analyst, predicted when different states would legalize same-sex marriage in the future. He looked at the percentage of people voting to ban same-sex marriage in the most recent poll in each state and the proportion of people who said religion was important in their day-to-day lives. He then assumed that each year there will be 2 per cent fewer voters who want to ban same-sex marriage, based on the trend in US states that have now legalized same-sex marriage.

Using these methods, Silver predicted that half of the states would vote against marriage bans by 2012. He further predicted that the last ten states to drop the ban would all be in the conservative south of the country (including Kentucky, Alabama and Mississippi) between 2019 and 2024. It remains to be seen how successful this prediction will be.

Transforming society

The world is changing fast in many ways. At the start of the twentieth century black people, women and people with disabilities lived as second-class citizens with few or no voting rights and restricted freedom. At that time homosexuality was still almost universally illegal. A lot has changed since then, but it was not until the 1990s that same-sex unions were first legalized in some parts of the world. The concept of marriage has been rapidly changing. The world has moved on from a situation when marriages between people of different races were unacceptable, through acceptance of divorce, to same-sex marriage. Our ideas of what makes a family now include not only a man, a woman and their children, but also homosexual and transgender parents, test-tube babies and children born from surrogate mothers.

case study

Argentina moves forward

At 4:05 am on July 15, 2010, hundreds of people waiting in the cold outside Argentina's Congress building in Buenos Aires heard that the Senate had approved same-sex marriage by 33 votes to 27. The law confirms Argentina as a leader in gay rights, despite strong opposition from the Roman Catholic Church. The evening before the vote, 60,000 people took part in a march on Congress, organized by the Church, carrying orange flags symbolizing opposition to the bill. Argentinians have religious freedom but Catholicism is the official religion and this has an impact on laws in the country, such as making abortion illegal. For many Argentinians the vote in favor of same-sex marriage is proof that the country is moving forward. As Cesar Cigliutti, president of the Argentine Homosexual Community, put it: "This is encouraging not just for our couples, but also because it is Argentine society valuing diversity."

▼ The banner held by supporters of same-sex marriage in Argentina reads "The same love, the same rights, with the same name."

▲ In March 2010, ten same-sex couples were married in the same ceremony in Washington, DC, after the nation's capital began recognizing same-sex marriage.

The reason that same-sex marriage is being debated at all is that the leaders around the world increasingly value human rights, even when these are at odds with traditional cultural and religious views. It is every individual's right in a place to have the same rights as others, including the right to express his or her own beliefs, to achieve happiness, health and stability, and to get married. More and more people each year believe that a person's sexual orientation should not affect this.

It's a fact

Webster's Dictionary, 1913 on marriage: "The act of marrying, or the state of being married; legal union of a man and a woman for life, as husband and wife; wedlock; matrimony."

Merriam-Webster Dictionary, online edition, 2003: "(1) The state of being united to a person of the opposite sex as husband or wife in a consensual and contractual relationship recognized by law; (2) the state of being united to a person of the same sex in a relationship like that of a traditional marriage."

Timeline

1967   US Supreme Court strikes down a Virginia law against inter-racial marriage in the case of Richard and Mildred Loving.

Private meetings between gay adults becomes legal in the UK.

1969   Stonewall riots in New York spark the gay rights movement.

1970   Jack Baker and Jim McConnell unsuccessfully apply for a wedding licence in Minnesota.

1973   American Psychiatric Association rules that homosexuality cannot be classified as a mental illness.

1980   Discrimination against homosexuals becomes illegal in the US.

1987   Mock mass same-sex wedding takes place in Washington to highlight the tax benefits that same-sex couples are denied.

1989   Denmark becomes the first country to legalize same-sex partnerships.

2000   Vermont legalizes first same-sex unions in the US.

2001   Germany's and the Netherlands' first gay weddings take place.

2003   Parts of Canada and Massachusetts, USA, legalize same-sex marriage.

2004   Officials in California and Oregon start to issue wedding licences to same-sex couples, but public pressure forces a change back to illegal status.

UK recognizes equal legal rights for same-sex couples and heterosexual couples joined in civil ceremonies.

2005   Spain, South Africa and Canada legalize same-sex marriage.

Pope John Paul calls same-sex marriage "evil."

2008   California overturns ban on gay marriage then bans it once more the following year – Proposition 8.

2009   Iowa, Vermont, Maine, legalize same-sex marriage.

India declassifies homosexuality as a mental illness.

2010   New Hampshire, legalizes same-sex marriage; California courts battle over the legality of Proposition 8.

2011 New York legalizes same-sex marriage, the largest state at the time to do so.

Glossary

Anglican   Member of the Church of England, part of the Christian church.

Annul   State officially that something is not valid any more.

Apartheid   Political system in South Africa from 1948 and 1994 in which black people had fewer civil rights than white people and had to live apart and use separate buses, schools and restaurants.

Chaste   State of not having sex with anyone or only with the person you are married to.

Civil partnership/union   Same-sex relationship recognized by the government of a country or region to have equal legal status as the marriage between a man and woman.

Contraception   Ways of preventing a woman from becoming pregnant including the use of condoms or pills. Contraception is sometimes called birth control.

Co-parenting   When parents are not married, living together or in a sexual relationship but share the responsibility of raising children.

Custody   Legal right or duty to take care of a child.

Donor insemination   When a man agrees to give sperm to be inserted by doctors into the womb of a woman, hopefully to make her pregnant.

Evangelical   Persuading others that Christian beliefs are the most important beliefs and that they should take on the Christian faith.

Hepatitis   Disease of the liver caused by

eating infected food or having contact with infected blood.

HIV/AIDS HIV is a virus that weakens the human immune system and AIDS is a range of symptoms often resulting in death that can result from HIV infection.

Inter-racial Between two races, sometimes used to describe relationships between black and white people.

Legal system Way of interpreting and enforcing laws distinctive to a particular country, region or place.

Natural law Basic principle that governs interactions between people, such as respect and fairness.

Next-of-kin status Legal authorization of being closely related to or responsible for someone else. Next-of-kin can take part in decisions about the person, such as whether they should have medical treatment or where they should live.

Nuclear family Consisting of mother, father and children and considered a basic unit making up societies.

Persecute To treat others cruelly or unfairly, often based on race, sexual orientation or political views.

Pink pound/dollar Describes the wealth of or business resulting from the homosexual community.

Plaintiff Person making a formal complaint against something or someone in a law court.

Sacred text Writings considered holy as they are connected with God, and that are significant for religious people.

Sanction To give official permission for something to happen.

Secular Unconnected with religious or spiritual matters.

Self-harm To deliberately cut or otherwise injure yourself as a result of having emotional or mental difficulties.

Sexual orientation Whether you are homosexual, heterosexual or bisexual.

Shaman A spiritual and physical healer in some societies.

STD Sexually transmitted disease such as HIV or syphilis.

Surrogacy When a woman gives birth to a baby for another person who cannot have children.

Visitation rights Official legal permission for a parent (or grandparent) to visit a child (grandchild) they normally don't look after, for example following divorce, separation or death of its parents.

Further Reading

Books:

Gay Marriage (Introducing Issues with Opposing Viewpoints) Lauri Friedman, editor (Greenhaven Press, 2009)

Sexual Orientation and Society (Issues Series vol. 153) Lisa Firth (Independence Educational Publishers, 2008)

Same-sex Marriage: Moral Wrong or Civil Right? Tricia Andryszewski (Twenty-First Century Books, 2007)

Web sites

Due to the changing nature of Internet links, Rosen Publishing has developed an online list of Web sites related to the subject of this book. This site is regularly updated. Please use this link to access the list:

http://www.rosenlinks.com/etde/same

Index

j326
D73t

THE TURNING TIDE

WILDER BRANCH LIBRARY
7140 E. SEVEN MILE RD.
DETROIT, MI 48234

MAY -- 2001